The Ten Commandments

The Liberating Rules of God

STUART BRISCOE

FISHERMAN
BIBLE STUDY SERIES

The Ten Commandments

PUBLISHED BY WATERBROOK PRESS
12265 Oracle Boulevard, Suite 200
Colorado Springs, Colorado 80921

All Scripture quotations, unless otherwise indicated, are taken from the *Holy Bible, New International Version* ®. NIV®. Copyright © 1973, 1978, 1984 by International Bible Society. Used by permission of Zondervan Publishing House. All rights reserved.

ISBN: 978-0-87788-803-1

Published in the United States by WaterBrook Multnomah, an imprint of the Crown Publishing Group, a division of Random House Inc., New York.

Printed in the United States of America
2009

15 14 13 12 11

Contents

How to Use This Studyguide

isherman studyguides are based on the inductive approach to Bible study. Inductive study is discovery study; we discover what the Bible says as we ask questions about its content and search for answers. This is quite different from the process in which a teacher *tells* a group *about* the Bible—what it means and what to do about it. In inductive study, God speaks directly to each of us through his Word.

A group functions best when a leader keeps the discussion on target, but the leader is neither the teacher nor the "answer person." A leader's responsibility is to *ask*—not *tell.* The answers come from the text itself as group members examine, discuss, and think together about the passage.

There are four kinds of questions in each study. The first is an *approach question.* Asked and answered before the Bible passage is read, this question breaks the ice and helps you start thinking about the topic of the Bible study. It begins to reveal where thoughts and feelings need to be transformed by Scripture.

Some of the earlier questions in each study are *observation questions*—who, what, where, when, and how—designed to help you learn some basic facts about the passage of Scripture.

Once you know what the Bible says, you need to ask, *What does it mean?* These *interpretation questions* help you discover the writer's basic message.

Next come *application questions,* which ask, *What does it mean to me?* They challenge you to live out the Scripture's life-transforming message.

Fisherman studyguides provide spaces between questions for jotting down responses as well as any related questions you would like to raise in the group. Each group member should have a copy of the studyguide and may take a turn in leading the group.

A group should use any accurate, modern translation of the Bible such as the *New International Version,* the *New American Standard Bible,* the *New Living Translation,* the *New Revised Standard Version,* the *New Jerusalem Bible,* or the *Good News Bible.* (Other translations or paraphrases of the Bible may be referred to when additional help is needed.) Bible commentaries should not be brought to a Bible study because they tend to dampen discussion and keep people from thinking for themselves.

Suggestions for Group Leaders

1. Thoroughly read and study the Bible passage before the meeting. Get a firm grasp on its themes and begin applying its teachings for yourself. Pray that the Holy Spirit will "guide you into all truth" (John 16:13) so that your leadership will guide others.

2. If any of the studyguide's questions seem ambiguous or unnatural to you, rephrase them, feeling free to add others that seem necessary to bring out the meaning of a verse.

3. Begin (and end) the study promptly. Start by asking someone to pray that every participant will both understand the passage and be open to its transforming power. Remember, the Holy Spirit is the teacher, not you!

4. Ask for volunteers to read the passages aloud.

5. As you ask the studyguide's questions in sequence, encourage everyone to participate in the discussion. If some are silent, try gently suggesting, "Let's have an answer from someone who hasn't spoken up yet."

6. If a question comes up that you can't answer, don't be afraid to admit that you're baffled. Assign the topic as a research project for someone to report on next week, or say, "I'll do some studying and let you know what I find out."

7. Keep the discussion moving, but be sure it stays focused. Though a certain number of tangents are inevitable, you'll want to quickly bring the discussion back to the topic at hand. Also, learn to pace the discussion so that you finish the lesson in the time allotted.

8. Don't be afraid of silences; some questions take time to answer, and some people need time to gather courage to speak. If silence persists, rephrase your question, but resist the temptation to answer it yourself.

9. If someone comes up with an answer that is clearly illogical or unbiblical, ask for further clarification: "What verse suggests that to you?"

10. Discourage overuse of cross references. Learn all you can from the passage at hand, while selectively incorporating a few important references suggested in the studyguide.

11. Some questions are marked with a ✐. This indicates that further information is available in the Leader's Notes at the back of the guide.

12. For more information on getting a new Bible study group started and keeping it functioning effectively, read *You Can Start a Bible Study Group* by Gladys M. Hunt and *Pilgrims in Progress: Growing Through Groups* by Jim and Carol Plueddemann. (Both books are available from Shaw Books.)

Suggestions for Group Members

1. Learn and apply the following ground rules for effective Bible study. (If new members join the group later, review these guidelines with the whole group.)

2. Remember that your goal is to learn all you can *from the Bible passage being studied.* Let it speak for itself without using Bible commentaries or other Bible passages. There is more than enough in each assigned passage to keep your group productively occupied for one session. Sticking to the passage saves the group from insecurity ("I don't have the right reference books—or the time to read anything else.") and confusion ("Where did *that* come from? I thought we were studying _____.").

3. Avoid the temptation to bring up those fascinating tangents that don't really grow out of the passage you are discussing. If the topic is of common interest, you can bring it up later in informal conversation after the study. Meanwhile, help one another stick to the subject.

4. Encourage one another to participate. People remember best what they discover and verbalize for

themselves. Some people are naturally shy, while others may be afraid of making a mistake. If your discussion is free and friendly and you show real interest in what other group members think and feel, the quieter ones will be more likely to speak up. Remember, the more people involved in a discussion, the richer it will be.

5. Guard yourself from answering too many questions or talking too much. Give others a chance to share their ideas. If you are one who participates easily, discipline yourself by counting to ten before you open your mouth.

6. Make personal, honest applications and commit yourself to letting God's Word change you.

Introduction

Playing by the rules isn't a popular idea today. This is apparent, judging by the distaste for authority and a prevailing sense of aimlessness in our individual and corporate lives. The confusion and hopelessness in our society relate directly to the lack of agreement that there *are* principles or rules to live by—things we should do and ways to do them. Whose "rules" do we follow anyway? I believe that in the Ten Commandments, God has succinctly spelled out some guidelines for us.

When God brought his chosen people out of Egypt, he established a covenant with them. He would be their God, and they would be his people. He wanted to work through them in all the surrounding nations, demonstrating what it meant to have a relationship with him. The Israelites would love the Lord their God with all their heart and mind and soul and strength, and they would love their neighbors as themselves. God gave them four commandments to help them show that God was first in their lives and six more to help them know how to love their neighbors. Those actions would show that they were God's unique people.

Today, thousands of years after God introduced these commandments, what should they mean to us? Do the Ten Commandments have any significance for the Christian today? Yes, not as a means of earning salvation but as a way of *demonstrating* that we have been saved through Christ. Do the commandments have any relevance to the non-Christian—the person on the street? Yes, because they provide ethical and moral principles designed for our well-being.

In today's anything-goes world, we need these rules to live by more than ever. They provide a bridle of restraint on wrong and hurtful actions, and they serve as a barometer of our love and respect for God. They act as a much-needed mirror, showing us the reality of our sin and our need, and as a guardian that can lead us to Christ for forgiveness and grace.

Who needs the Ten Commandments? We all do. Take time out to learn what it means to live by God's rules.

Putting God First

You Shall Have No Other Gods Before Me

DEUTERONOMY 5:1-7; 6:1-6; JOSHUA 24:14-24

I n this sophisticated, rational, and technological society, it's easy to push God more and more into the background as we follow after the dominant values and mentality of our age. In order to combat this tendency within us, God has made some powerful statements about himself in the Ten Commandments in which he reveals who he is and that he will not accept anything less than first place in our lives.

When the children of Israel entered the land of Canaan, God warned that they would find competition for their faith—false "gods" who would try to take his place. He tried to prepare the Israelites for the different cultures and religious structures they would encounter, and he warned them to live as the unique people of God.

1. What are some "gods" in our society that have particular appeal to you? Explain.

   Acceptance

READ DEUTERONOMY 5:1-7.

↗ 2. Of what did Moses remind the people of Israel as
they were poised to enter the Promised Land?

Who had saved them

3. Why do you suppose that God brought up past
history when identifying himself (verse 6)?

Reminder, Seeking appreciation

4. Why do you think he prefaced the command in
verse 7 with the remembrance in verse 6?

He felt He had to remind them

5. Think about what God has done for you in the
past, and complete the statement for yourself: "I
am the Lord your God, who has…" *thru grace
guides me thru many dangers, toils
& snares*

READ DEUTERONOMY 6:1-6.

6. What additional reasons did Moses give for the
   people to keep God's commands?

   For long life

7. Given the religious environment in which the
   Israelites lived, why do you think God's revelation
   emphasized that he is one (verse 4)?

   No other nation worship our God

8. What do you think it means to love God in the way
   prescribed in verse 5?

   Explain in Vs 6 -7 · 8

   What is one way you can show this kind of love
   for God?

   On mind 24/7

READ JOSHUA 24:14-24.

9. The Israelites just conquered the land of Canaan. What choices did they need to make in this new context (verses 14-15)?

What God they would serve

What past and present pressures did they face?

they were up setting society in new lands

10. The Israelites' history was full of demonstrations of God's graciousness and power on their behalf (verses 17-18). With this history and all of the people's good intentions, why do you think Joshua was so insistent that they choose again to serve the Lord alone (see verses 19-23)?

11. Joshua warned the people against religious syncretism—adding the local gods to their faith in the Lord. What's the difference between being syncretistic (combining and reconciling differing beliefs) and being tolerant of other religions?

Dnt join them

Living by the Rules

12.   In your present situation, do you relate more closely
      with the struggles of the people of Israel or with
      Joshua's allegiance (verse 15)? Explain.

13.   In what way(s) are you prone to syncretism? What
      do you need to "throw away" in order to serve God
      and put him first in your life?

Surely not tolerance

STUDY 2

No Idols Allowed

You Shall Not Make for Yourself an Idol

EXODUS 20:4-6; JEREMIAH 10:1-16

The children of Israel faced cultural pressure to pay homage to local, man-made false deities. Idolatry is not so clear-cut in our Western society today. It's easy for Christians to feel superior to religions that use images or articles as objects of worship. We don't bow down to any images, so we relax, thinking that here's at least one commandment we can easily keep.

But idols can take nonreligious forms too, and we face pressures to replace the intangible reality of God with more tangible things. Money, status, our families, our careers—these things vie with God for our allegiance. In his book *Idols for Destruction*, Herbert Schlossberg said, "Anyone with a hierarchy of values has placed something at its apex, and whatever that is, is the God he serves."

1. What's at the top of your list of values—the thing that's most important to you? Why is this most important to you?

READ EXODUS 20:4-6.

2. State the second commandment briefly in your own words without using the words *idol* or *God.*

3. How does this second commandment expand on the first commandment in verse 3?

4. Why do you think God reacted so strongly against idolatry (verse 5)?

How do you respond to this picture of God's jealousy?

5. What is a promised result of a life committed to the one true God?

6. When, if ever, have you seen the effects of following or not following God passed on in families?

⚡7. What would you say to someone who states, "I can't believe in a God who punishes people like this"?

READ JEREMIAH 10:1-16.

8. What strikes you most about idols as they are described in this passage?

9. Even though they are frauds, why are idols (any image, person, or value that replaces God) and what they represent still so appealing to people?

10. Compare the descriptive names used for God throughout this passage with the descriptions of the pagan idols.

✍ 11. What damage can idolatry of any kind do to your spiritual life?

Living by the Rules

12. What are some of your own "idols"—those people, things, or desires that have become more important to you than God?

13. Which ideas or reminders in these passages will best help you in your struggle against idolatry?

Honoring God's Name

*You Shall Not Misuse the Name
of the Lord Your God*

EXODUS 20:7; 3:1-15

P roverbs says that a good name is to be desired more than riches. But what's in a name? "When I tell somebody my name," Frederick Buechner observed, "I have given him a hold over me that he didn't have before. If he calls it out, I stop, look, and listen whether I want to or not." A name is a powerful thing, representing the reputation and character of the person who bears it. This was especially true in Old Testament times.

When God gave his name to Moses, he took the initiative to reveal something more about himself than had previously been known. In effect, he was saying, "I'm knowable. I want to introduce myself to you." In giving us his name, God gives us an understanding of himself that we did not have before. We can never know all of who God is, but we have a glimpse of his true character and being through his name, and we must be careful to cherish and honor what it represents.

1. If your name were different, do you think you would be different? Why or why not?

READ EXODUS 20:7.

✐2. "Taking the name of the Lord in vain" is a better-known translation of this commandment. To take something *in vain* means "to empty of content; to make irrelevant." Describe a time when you, or someone else, subtly emptied the Lord's name of meaning or made it irrelevant.

3. What does the idea of *misusing* God's name add to your understanding of this commandment?

4. Does misusing God's name only include swearing and profanity? Why or why not?

Read Exodus 3:1-15.

5. How did God identify himself at first to Moses (verses 5-6)?

6. What more do we learn about God's character from his words in verses 7-9?

7. Note Moses's two objections to his new assignment. What do these objections tell us about him?

    How might God's answers have been a comfort to Moses?

8. If God had given you a similar task, what questions would you have asked?

    Would you have been satisfied with God's answers in this passage? Explain.

9. What more did Moses learn about God from the name he revealed in verses 14 and 15?

10. What is the significance of a God who reveals his name to people as opposed to false gods that are named by people?

Living by the Rules

11. How does the fact that you, as a Christian, bear God's name influence your behavior?

12. Colossians 3:17 says, "And whatever you do, whether in word or deed, do it all in the name of the Lord Jesus." What can you do to honor God's name in word and deed this week?

Keeping the Sabbath

Remember the Sabbath Day
by Keeping It Holy

EXODUS 20:8-11; 31:12-17; MARK 2:23–3:6

Keeping the Sabbath. In today's driven, entertainment-saturated society, this sounds like an impossible, old-fashioned idea. If we think about it at all, we usually operate on the basis of what we want to do with our leisure time, or we simply follow the tradition in which we were raised. That's a far cry from thinking the issues through and coming to a conclusion before the Lord as to what we ought to do on a Sabbath day.

After bringing the Israelites out of slavery in Egypt, God instituted a Sabbath day for the people. Obviously, our circumstances are different from theirs. They were runaway slaves from Egypt, a nomadic people wandering in the desert. Their workday was quite different from ours. But regardless of the situation, God recognized the human need to rest and regain perspective. We can demonstrate our relationship to God by the choices we make about how we do our work and, maybe more important, by what we do when we are not working.

1. What Sabbath traditions, if any, did you grow up with?

READ EXODUS 20:8-11 AND 31:12-17.

✐ 2. On what event is the Sabbath concept based?

3. What other reasons are cited in 31:16-17 for the Israelites to keep a Sabbath day?

4. Note the emphasis on keeping the Sabbath holy. The Hebrew word for "holy" means "to set apart." Discuss some ways we can make an otherwise normal day "holy."

5. What does this command implicitly say to us about work and our attitude toward it (20:8-11)?

How does this perspective compare to our society's view of work today?

6. Do you think keeping the Sabbath means only that we cease our labor? Discuss.

What does the aspect of *celebrating* (31:16) add to your idea of keeping the Sabbath?

READ MARK 2:23–3:6.

7. By New Testament times, Jewish Sabbath laws had become meticulous and burdensome. Judging from the two events described in this passage, what were some of the things that were not allowed on the Sabbath?

8. How do Jesus's actions and words shed new light on what the Sabbath is all about?

✐ 9.   The Pharisees and teachers may have been earnestly seeking to be obedient to the Sabbath command, but how were they missing the point?

✐ 10.   Did Jesus negate the fourth commandment with his words and actions? Why or why not?

Living by the Rules

11.   With the previous scriptures in mind, how do you now define what it means to keep the Sabbath today?

12.   Close by reading Isaiah 58:13-14. What attitudes do you need to cultivate in order to honor the Sabbath principle in your life?

Honoring the Family

Honor Your Father and Your Mother

SELECTIONS FROM RUTH

lvin Toffler, in his book *Future Shock*, predicted that the family will "break up and shatter and then come together again in weird ways." Some of the weird ways he suggested were parents shopping at "embryo emporiums" to choose a child, and then hiring "professional parents" to care for them. There will be serial marriages, with spouses one after the other, producing aggregate families of "semisiblings" as well, Toffler surmised in his futuristic scenario. One look around and we can see Toffler's predictions are not too far off.

Any talk of honoring parents is empty unless we take the changes in our society concerning family and marriage seriously. What does this fifth command really mean for us, especially if we don't know who our parents are, don't know them well, or don't live close enough to express appreciation? A look at the changes experienced by one family in the Bible may give us some clues about how to honor our parents, and what "family" can mean in various situations.

1. Do you think the family is doomed to extinction, as some sociologists say? Why or why not?

READ RUTH 1:1-22.

  2. What family system was in effect at the beginning of this story (verses 1-4)?

What "family" was operating at the end of chapter 1?

3. List some of the family changes Ruth experienced at this time in her life.

What did Naomi's people and family offer her?

READ RUTH 3:1-9; 4:9-10,13-17.

4. What additional facts can you gather about how families operated in this time and culture?

5. How do you know that Ruth respected and honored Naomi?

How do you know Naomi appreciated Ruth?

6. How was Naomi honored late in her life (4:13-17)?

7. In what ways is this family a good example of loving relationships?

8. Identify some reasons the Bible gives for honoring our parents:

    Exodus 20:12

    Ephesians 6:1-3

    Colossians 3:12-14,20

    What other reasons can you think of?

9. Based on this study, what aspects of God's intentions for the family do you think have *not* changed since this command was given?

10. What can happen in a family when the parents are not honored or respected? Give examples from Scripture or from families you know.

Living by the Rules

11. What might the command "Honor your father and your mother" mean to someone who is from a troubled or nontraditional family?

12. In your particular family situation, what does this command mean to you?

What is one way you can honor your parents?

Valuing Life

You Shall Not Murder

EXODUS 21:12-14; LEVITICUS 19:16-18; PSALM 139:1-16

In these four simple, straightforward words, God confronts us with a complex idea that requires our best thinking about the nature of human beings and the significance of life. Some people tell us that human beings are highly developed animals, and we certainly are. But if these people also mean that human beings are *only* highly developed animals, we must disagree. Scripture tells us that human life is sacred because people are made in the image and likeness of God. Purposeful destruction of what God has made in his image—out of vengeance or malice or premeditation—defies God's authority and ignores the tremendous value he puts on his creation.

1. What evidence do you see in our society that indicates a valuing or devaluing of life?

READ EXODUS 21:12-14.

   ✐ 2. What distinctions did God make regarding killing and murder?

   ✐ 3. Why do you think the punishment was so severe for this crime?

   ✐ 4. Does God's command to punish the murderer with death go against his own commandment to not murder? Why or why not?

READ LEVITICUS 19:16-18.

   5. List the "do nots" in Leviticus 19. How could these prohibitions protect and enhance life within a civilization?

⌀ 6. Which of these "do nots" involve attitudes and which are actions?

How can our attitudes sometimes lead us to wrong actions?

7. What do you think God's statement "I am the LORD" has to do with these commands (verses 16,18)?

READ PSALM 139:1-16.

⌀ 8. What aspects of God's character are revealed in this passage?

9. What is implied about human life if God is this personally involved with us?

10. What evidence that God values life do you find in all of the previous passages?

Living by the Rules

11. How has this study affected your own views on the value of life?

✐ 12. If there is time, discuss how the biblical view of the sanctity of life affects your position on one of these related issues:

capital punishment

abortion

suicide

war

Preserving Marriage

You Shall Not Commit Adultery

1 CORINTHIANS 6:12-20; 7:1-6; MATTHEW 5:27-30

W hen we see a Do Not Enter sign, something in our human nature makes us want to enter immediately. But when we see the word "Explosives" by it, we realize that there was a very good reason for the negative command. Positive statements lie behind God's negative commandments, too, showing God's deep concern for our well-being in all areas of life.

The seventh commandment shows God's concern for marriage. Adultery not only defies God but also destroys families and degrades people. We can't stop the sexually attractive things that bombard us every day in our society. But as Martin Luther said, "You can't stop the birds from flying over your head, but you can stop them from nesting in your hair." If we begin to call our lust and desire sin, we can begin to understand the attractiveness of this sin and learn to avoid it.

1. Why do people commit adultery?

READ 1 CORINTHIANS 6:12-20.

    ✐ 2.   Immorality was a problem for the Corinthians. The thrust of Paul's argument to the church is given in verses 18-20. What reasons did he cite for instructing the Corinthians to flee from sexual immorality?

    ✐ 3.   What were Paul's objections to the Corinthians' slogans that they used to justify their behavior (verses 12-13)?

    ✐ 4.   What does it mean that our bodies are "for the Lord" (verse 13)?

    ✐ 5.   What "price" was Paul referring to in verse 20? (See 1 Corinthians 6:11 and Romans 4:25.)

        How does this fact strengthen Paul's argument for sexual purity?

READ 1 CORINTHIANS 7:1-6.

6. What is another safeguard against adultery that Paul discussed here?

7. How do you respond to Paul's statement that sex is a marital duty?

What is the rationale for this statement (verse 4)?

8. Paul encouraged a mutual respect and communication between a husband and wife concerning sexual matters. How might this discourage adultery?

READ MATTHEW 5:27-30.

9. How did Jesus extend this seventh commandment?

10. What is the underlying principle behind his answer to the problem?

11. In what ways do these passages support the value and sanctity of marriage?

Living by the Rules

12. Whether you are married or single, what does it mean to honor God with your body in a society of unrestrained sex?

13. What encouragement would you offer to those who have suffered on either side of adultery?

Keeping Property in Perspective

You Shall Not Steal

1 TIMOTHY 6:3-19

A Gallup poll that asked people questions about their expense accounts, income taxes, and so on, found that a high percentage of businesspeople did not regard cheating on these items as "stealing." This attitude was evident in both people who attended church and those who did not. George Gallup concluded that many people in our culture who claim to have an interest in religion do not let it affect their own morality or behavior.

The eighth commandment is short and simple but not at all simplistic. What is it really getting at? Like those people polled, most of us have an inadequate view of what constitutes stealing. Paul's advice to Timothy about contentment and godliness will help us explore our own attitudes toward money and property and will help us keep things in perspective.

1. Have you ever been the victim of theft? How did it make you feel?

   Have you ever stolen anything? How did it make you feel?

READ 1 TIMOTHY 6:3-10.

2. Compare the "godliness" of these false teachers with the true godliness that Paul described (verses 3-8).

3. What dangers are inherent in discontentment and financial greed (verses 9-10)?

   Discuss some of the temptations you have faced in this area.

4. How is Paul's teaching in verses 6-8 an antidote for these dangers?

5. How can we steal from others in ways that don't involve money or property?

In what sense is stealing from others also stealing from God?

READ 1 TIMOTHY 6:11-19.

6. From what did Paul instruct Timothy to "flee" (verse 11)?

7. List the strong verbs Paul used in verses 11-14 to exhort Timothy. Which of these actions do you need to pursue most right now in your fight of the faith?

8. From Paul's comments in verses 17 and 18, and previously in verses 9 and 10, how do you know that money in itself is not evil?

✐ 9. Instead of wanting to get richer, how are we to use our property and wealth? Why?

Living by the Rules

10. What overall principles do you find in this passage to help you fight the temptation to steal on any level?

11. Reread Paul's blessing of God in 1 Timothy 6:15-16. How can having this view of God affect your perspective on the material things of this life?

Speaking the Truth

*You Shall Not Give False Testimony
Against Your Neighbor*

EPHESIANS 4:17-32

Not wanting to insult a fellow member of parliament, Winston Churchill once accused him not of lying but of "perpetrating a terminological inexactitude." We dress up lying in many ways. We excuse it, philosophize about it, and cover up the truth. But a lie is still a lie. And lying undermines much of what holds our society together.

This commandment expresses a positive concern in negative terms. Forbidding the giving of false testimony against one's neighbor expresses God's desire for his people to love and examine the truth. Although we might think of this verse in terms of testimony in a court of law, the Scriptures make it clear that God by no means limits it to that context. He wants all of our relationships to be characterized by truth and righteousness.

1. Imagine a society with no safeguards or restrictions for honesty and truth (in legal systems, financial and

credit systems, consumer transactions, relationships, and so on). What would such a society be like?

READ EPHESIANS 4:17-24.

2. What repercussions did the Gentiles' futile thinking have on their quality of life?

3. What seems to have been at the core of their darkened understanding (verse 18)?

    How would this root problem lead to wrong thinking?

4. What are some futile ways of thinking you have observed in our culture today?

5. On what basis did Paul entreat the Ephesian Christians to live differently than the Gentiles (verses 20-24)?

✐ 6. Paul assumed that in knowing Jesus, we can know the truth (verse 21). Discuss how knowing the truth in Jesus can help us break the cycle of darkened and false thinking.

7. What is involved in "putting off" our "old self" (verses 22-24)?

How can you pursue this? Be practical and specific.

8. What do you think is our part and what is God's part in "putting on" the new self?

READ EPHESIANS 4:25-32.

9. To what does the "therefore" in verse 25 refer? What was Paul's point?

✐ 10. Note the "do nots" in verses 26-30. What does *not* speaking the truth do to our relationships with others and with God?

Living by the Rules

✐ 11. According to this passage, what is our primary means of living a truthful life (verses 22-23)?

12. What situation, if any, are you facing right now that requires a commitment to telling the truth? How can you speak the truth in love?

Being Content

You Shall Not Covet

EXODUS 20:17-21; PHILIPPIANS 4:10-20

In the original draft of the Declaration of Independence, Thomas Jefferson wrote that all people had the inalienable rights to life, liberty, and the pursuit of *possessions.* The wording was changed eventually to *happiness,* but our thinking hasn't changed at all. We all feel that our happiness lies mostly with the things we have. If we believe that happiness can be found in our possessions, then to be more happy, we will want more things, and we will quickly exploit others in order to get them. Chances are we don't even realize the underlying greed and covetousness that often motivate our pursuit of possessions. In this final commandment, God addressed what is in our hearts and, in so doing, gives us another standard for true happiness and contentment.

1. In what ways have you been tempted to "keep up with the Joneses" lately?

READ EXODUS 20:17-21.

✐ 2. Review all of the commandments in Exodus 20:1-16. How does covetousness pervade many of them?

3. What aspects of life are represented in the listing in verse 17?

Why do you suppose God spelled out these particulars for this commandment and not for others?

✐ 4. What did God hope would be the result of his revelation to the Israelites (verse 20)?

Explain the difference between being afraid of God and "fearing God," as it's meant in this passage.

Read Philippians 4:10-20.

5. Paul was in prison in Rome when he wrote this letter. What might he have been tempted to covet?

✎ 6. What factors contributed to Paul's "secret" of being content in any and every situation?

7. Are contentment and covetousness mutually exclusive attitudes? Why or why not?

8. How does your contentment level compare with Paul's?

What can you learn from this passage to help you be more content with what you have?

9. Read Matthew 6:19-21. How does Jesus's teaching here encourage you in your battle against the sin of covetousness?

Living by the Rules

10. Have the Ten Commandments become more real or understandable to you during the course of this study? Explain.

11. What area of your life do you foresee being most affected by your renewed understanding of the Ten Commandments? Explain.

Closing Thoughts

You may have realized during this study that there is no way any of us can possibly keep all of these commandments all the time. So what's the point of studying them if we can never truly please God by keeping them? Because in order to change our hearts, God must show us our need. These commandments clearly show us our sin. When we can admit how far we fall short of what God requires, we are ready to accept his provision for our sin through Jesus Christ's death and resurrection.

So take heart. If you are struggling to integrate all the truths of this study into your life, always keep in mind that God's grace is never ending and that "there is now no condemnation for those who are in Christ Jesus, because through Christ Jesus the law of the Spirit of life set [us] free from the law of sin and death" (Romans 8:1-2).

Leader's Notes

STUDY 1: PUTTING GOD FIRST

Question 2. Horeb refers to Mount Sinai, where God gave Moses the Ten Commandments and other laws. See Exodus 19–20.

Question 7. This statement in Deuteronomy 6:4 is known as the Hebrew *Shema,* recited twice daily by devout Jews. God said he is the one and only, the absolutely unique God. He showed the Israelites that he is greater than all other gods when he overcame the gods of Egypt. (See Exodus 7–14.) When God claims to be "one," it also means there is a unity in his Person. The false gods of other nations contradicted themselves, and if you pleased one god, then you could be upsetting another god. But the Lord is one and does not contradict or fight against himself. He is completely different and above all the false gods of other nations.

Question 9. Joshua was now the leader of the Israelites. Moses was not allowed to enter Canaan due to his disobedience. (See Numbers 20:1-13.) Moses's discourses in Deuteronomy were his farewell words.

Question 11. Syncretism means pulling a lot of divergent things together to make a whole out of them. This can be appealing, but in the process, the divergent things are mixed and lose their uniqueness. The children of Israel faced such a situation in Canaan. When they conquered a town, they captured the king and people, and they were tempted to gather up the gods of the town for themselves as well. The true God and his laws would get lost amid these other religions. And the worship of these other gods was often tied into sexual and sensual practices, which was not pleasing to God. The thrust of the first commandment is that God's uniqueness must be preserved and honored. You can respect other beliefs (tolerance) without embracing them.

STUDY 2: NO IDOLS ALLOWED

Question 4. We need to take God's attributes all together. The holiness of God is never separated from his jealousy, so he exhibits a holy jealousy and a jealous holiness. "*Zealous* might be a better translation in modern English, since jealousy has acquired an exclusively bad meaning.... *Jealousy* does not refer to an emotion so much as to an activity.... [It] is not to be seen as intolerance but exclusiveness, and it springs both from the uniqueness of God and the uniqueness of his relationship to Israel. No husband who truly loved his wife could endure to share her with another man: no more will God share Israel with a rival" (R. Alan Cole, *Exodus,* Tyndale Old Testament Commentary, Downers Grove, IL: InterVarsity Press, 1973, p. 156).

Question 7. As stated in note 4, we must remember to see God's attributes as a whole. If God is not just, then neither is he loving. Judgment is part of his love and holiness. The Hebrew word for "love" in Exodus 20:6 is *hesed,* meaning "love, mercy, grace, kindness." It is an all-encompassing covenant word. The structure of the Hebrew contrasts the punishment of "three or four generations" (denoting continuity) with the love shown to "thousands of generations" (indicating limitlessness). God acts firmly but also remains ready to act graciously, and his grace is always infinitely greater than his judgment.

Question 11. Idolatry turns means into an end; tangible things replace the intangible and become the focus. It makes things more important than people, and it places imagination above God's revelation, seeking to remake God into something we can "imagine." Idolatry imposes limits on God's transcendence, squishing God down into our box; it puts humans "in control" of their self-made god and fashions that god into a popular style. Finally, idolatry detracts from God's chosen image, denigrating who he is and who we are.

STUDY 3: HONORING GOD'S NAME

Question 2. People in Old Testament times understood the concept of using God's name in vain. The Israelites took oaths as part of their transactions, calling on the name of the Lord: "The Lord do so-and-so to me if I don't…" or "As the Lord lives…" These expressions showed their dependence on God to control the results of the promise. They took an oath that made God their judge. However, using God's name in this context without any real consideration of accountability to God could empty the oath, and God's name, of any meaning. We do this today when we engage in Christian activities "for the Lord" with selfish motives or when we pray "in Jesus's name" for things we just want for ourselves. By using God's name to manipulate situations or ignoring what his will may be, we empty his name of significance.

Question 9. "In the ancient world a name was not merely a label but was virtually equivalent to whoever or whatever bore it" (Walter Elwell, ed., *Evangelical Dictionary of Theology,* Grand Rapids: Baker, 1984, p. 750). In Hebrew, God's name is often linked with his being; thus, believing "in his name" is the same as believing in God himself.

The Hebrew syntax of Moses's question in Exodus 3:13—"What is his name?"—shows that he was inquiring more deeply into the quality or character of God revealed by his name. God then used his eternal covenant name of LORD or "Yahweh."

Question 10. God revealed himself here in stark contrast to the false gods all around the Israelites—gods that received their names from their human creators. As a human being gave a god its name, he also gave it personality, character, and a reputation. It all resulted from human ingenuity, a person imposing his wishes on his gods. But when God revealed his own name, he took the initiative and chose to let us know his true nature. He was saying, "You can't make me the way you want me to be. I AM, and I will demonstrate who I am."

STUDY 4: KEEPING THE SABBATH

Question 2. Creation is cited in both places as the basis for a Sabbath day of rest. (See Genesis 2:2-3.) God created in six days, and on the seventh day, he rested. He was refreshed and reflected on all he had done. He rejoiced in all he had achieved.

Deuteronomy 5:12-15 adds that the Sabbath was also a reminder of God's work on Israel's behalf. The Israelites were to remember with thanksgiving what God had done for them in saving them from slavery in Egypt.

Question 9. In an earnest effort to obey this command, the Jewish leaders became so obsessed with meticulous observation of the Sabbath that they ended up desecrating it. These Pharisees were going by the book, following the detailed definitions of what constituted "work" on the Sabbath as found in the *Mishnah* (the listing of oral laws in the *Talmud,* the source of Jewish law). One such law states that one could not wear false teeth on the Sabbath because that would constitute carrying a "burden." Another states that one could not travel more than a certain distance from home on the Sabbath. But if someone wanted to go farther than that, he would travel the Sabbath's day distance, find a tree, put food under it, and say that this was his new "home." Then he would travel another Sabbath's day journey from that point. In spelling out the rules, the religious leaders put themselves in a rut of legalism and often ended up manipulating the law.

Question 10. Jesus adhered to this commandment and worshiped regularly on the Sabbath. He also healed on the Sabbath. The authorities had determined that to heal was work, and one should not work on the Sabbath. Jesus answered this objection by saying that he himself fulfilled all that the original command prefigured. He was saying, "I govern the Sabbath; it doesn't govern me. Remember that the Sabbath was made *for* humanity. In it, God graciously provides an opportunity for rest, reflection, and the privilege of worship and obedience.

Enjoy it as a precious gift from God, and don't get too locked into rules and regulations."

STUDY 5: HONORING THE FAMILY

Question 2. The family clan in Old Testament times included not only husband, wife, and children, but a wide network of blood relations and in-laws. This support system was necessary for economic and emotional survival.

Question 4. The kinsman-redeemer was a relative responsible for ensuring the continuation of the extended family. See Ruth 2:1,20 and 4:2-8, as well as Deuteronomy 25:5-10, for further information.

Question 6. Ruth gave birth to a son, but Naomi was the one who was congratulated. She now had a "son" to carry on her husband's name. By putting the child on her lap, she symbolized that she was adopting the child. Naomi's joy and the women's praise were heartfelt, for widows who did not have kinsman-redeemers were left to live a life of poverty and want.

Question 11. Many people today are from single-parent homes or have been raised in abusive situations. Be sensitive to those in the group who may have had difficult family relationships.

STUDY 6: VALUING LIFE

Question 2. The sixth commandment is given in a general form, but Scripture clearly distinguishes between accidental killing and premeditated murder.

Question 3. Even here God was affirming the sanctity of life. The fact that this extreme punishment was given for murder shows just how important human life is to God. This Old Testament system of justice is known as *lex talionis,* "the law of retaliation." It didn't mean an "eye for an eye and a tooth for a tooth," as some have misinterpreted it. The system limited the retaliation you could receive: If you took someone else's eye out, the punishment meted out to you could not exceed the taking of your eye. In the same way, Genesis 9:6 provides a limitation. If someone sheds another person's blood, that first person's blood must be shed. And this is the reason: "For in the image of God has God made man."

Question 4. Earlier Bible translations used the word *kill* for the sixth commandment, whereas modern scholars have more accurately used the word *murder,* as the Hebrew word here implies violent killing. This commandment does not prohibit all killing as much as it prohibits premeditated murder (see Deuteronomy 20, which describes the limitations of killing in war, and Numbers 35, which describes cities of refuge for those who killed others accidentally).

Question 6. In his Sermon on the Mount, Jesus pinpointed the problem of evil, which lies in our hearts (Matthew 5:21-22). Each of us is capable of "killing" others with deadly hatred and selfishness as well as lashing out in deadly actions that stem from inner attitudes.

Question 8. God is all-knowing (omniscient), present everywhere (omnipresent), our Creator, infinite and sovereign, and personally involved with his creation.

Question 12. For an excellent discussion of these issues, see chapter 6 of Stuart Briscoe's book *The Ten Commandments: Playing by the Rules* (Colorado Springs: Shaw Books, 2000).

Study 7: Preserving Marriage

Question 2. The city of Corinth was known for its pagan worship, which included temple prostitution as well as other excesses. The apostle Paul wrote this letter to address some serious issues of sexual impurity and factions in the church (see 1 Corinthians 1–3; 5). "The instability of the Corinthians is not surprising in view of the novel tensions to which their utterly anti-Christian religious and moral environment exposed them" (Norman Hillyer, *The New Bible Commentary*, rev. ed., Grand Rapids: Eerdmans, 1970, p. 1049).

Question 3. The phrases Paul quoted—"Everything is permissible for me" and "Food for the stomach and the stomach for food"—may have been slogans often quoted by the Corinthians to justify their behavior, due to their "freedom" in the Lord or because sex is as natural a part of the body as eating is. But our freedom in the Lord must be balanced with wisdom, love, and discipline. (See Romans 14; 1 Corinthians 8; and Galatians 5:13-14.)

Question 4. For Paul, the body was much more than just the physical shell and was designed for much more than eating or physical pleasure. The Lord in us fulfills the purpose for which we were made, and we are his "temples" (1 Corinthians 6:19). Christ's death and resurrection and the resurrection of our bodies are also connected here, implying that "the present physical body must be properly valued and used. As a resurrected body it will still be needed for God's purposes" (Hillyer, *New Bible Commentary*, p. 1059).

Question 5. Jesus died for our sins and paid the ultimate price for our redemption and justification before God. Paul urges us to consider this and to honor God out of grateful hearts.

Question 10. Jesus used hyperbole here to make his point. If you are going to avoid getting into an illicit sexual relationship, you must discipline your life. Get rid of those things that tempt you. Avoid those things that pull you in. Make decisions about boundaries before you get into compromising situations. If we live uncurbed lives, our unfulfilled desires and uncertain standards will often lead to illicit relationships—in thought if not in deed.

Question 13. Of all the commandments, this one may be the most difficult for people to openly and honestly discuss. If there are any in your group who have been on either side of adultery, be sure to close the study with the reassurance of God's love and forgiveness. You might want to read John 8:1-11 as an example of Jesus's response to the sin and the sinner.

STUDY 8: KEEPING PROPERTY IN PERSPECTIVE

Question 4. Scripture teaches that property is necessary, and we need certain things, such as food, shelter, and clothes. Even though we need these things, our *ownership* is not an absolute right. We hold everything we have in trust as from the Lord. Keeping this perspective helps us be content with what we have.

Question 5. Stealing is much more than taking from another person what is not ours to take. We can also deprive others of their liberty through slavery or of their dignity by prejudice or injustice. We can steal from our employers by not putting in a full day's work or by "borrowing" paper and pens. Our institutions and corporations can also take advantage of the poor, using them to make a larger profit (see Isaiah 10:1-3). We can steal from God by living inconsistent lives: Loudly professing one thing and living another robs God of his credibility. We can also steal from God by refusing to give tithes and offerings (see Malachi 3:7-8). Since "the earth is the LORD's, and everything in it" (Psalm 24:1), when we steal from others, we are stealing what God has entrusted to them, and, thus, in a sense we are stealing from God as well.

Question 9. Paul addressed another aspect of this topic in Ephesians 4:28: "He who has been stealing must steal no longer, but must work, doing something useful with his own hands, that he may have something to share with those in need." The opposite of stealing is the blessing of hard work. The Bible does not promise us the "good life," financially. Instead, it says that we should produce in order to put ourselves in a position to give to others.

STUDY 9: SPEAKING THE TRUTH

Question 6. The truth that we come to know in Christ is that we are sinners and that he loves and forgives us. This realization enables us to stay open to God's work in our lives and not harden our hearts against his way of doing things. The Gentiles lacked true knowledge, and this ignorance of God separated them from him and led to indulgent living based on false thinking. The truth of salvation in Christ sheds light on our false thoughts and helps us keep perspective. True knowledge can then lead to truthful living.

Question 10. Being honest and open, in love, is a necessity if we are to live together and please God. Not speaking truthfully to others comes from our pride, our defensiveness, and wanting to hurt others, and this is sin. When we think and act with malice, anger, rage, and bitterness, we destroy ourselves. We not only destroy relationships by lying and deception, but we also grieve the Holy Spirit, who is also called the Spirit of truth (John 16:13). When we learn God's truth, we begin to love it. When we love the truth, then we can begin to live it with integrity.

Question 11. We can combat lying through our relationship with Christ. Jesus shows us the truth about ourselves and humankind. We must decide that truth is found in him, then recognize and repent of the untruth and deception that has become part and parcel of our lives.

STUDY 10: BEING CONTENT

Question 2. The Hebrew word for "covetousness" has the same root as the word for "desire" or "delight." Desires are fine, but covetousness is an inordinate, unfettered desire that can lead to dishonesty, injustice, exploitation of others, and an insatiable demand for more.

Question 4. We are often exhorted in Scripture to "fear the Lord," to approach him with a proper and reverential sense of awe. But God also tells us not to be afraid of him (to shrink back in alarm or fear of danger), for his intentions for us are good.

Question 6. Paul had learned that God could be trusted to meet his needs physically and financially and that God sometimes uses other people in this regard. God used the Philippians many times to aid Paul in times of need, not only financially, but also by sharing in his troubles (Philippians 4:14) and being partners in sharing the gospel (1:5). We can encourage one another toward contentment and trusting God more. For more background on Paul's relationship with the church in Philippi, see Acts 16:12-40 and 20:1,6.

The Fisherman Bible Studyguide Series— Get Hooked on Studying God's Word

Old Testament Studies

Genesis

Proverbs

Acts 1-12

Acts 13-28

Colossians

James

New Testament Studies

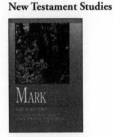

Mark

John

Romans

Philippians

1, 2, 3 John

Revelation

Women of the Word

Becoming Women of Purpose

Wisdom for Today's Woman

Women Like Us

Women Who Believed God

For more information, visit our Web site: www.waterbrookmultnomah.com

Topical Studies

Building Your House on the Lord

Discipleship

Encouraging Others

The Fruit of the Spirit

Growing Through Life's Challenges

Guidance and God's Will

Higher Ground

Lifestyle Priorities

The Parables of Jesus

Parenting with Purpose and Grace

Prayer

Proverbs & Parables

The Sermon on the Mount

Speaking Wisely

Spiritual Disciplines

Spiritual Gifts

Spiritual Warfare

The Ten Commandments

When Faith Is All You Have

Who Is the Holy Spirit?